Rhymes of Sinister Kinds

K Delaney

BookLeaf Publishing

Presentation by *BookLeaf Publishing*

Web: www.bookleafpub.com

E-mail: info@bookleafpub.com

ISBN: 9789357617079

First edition 2022

To you.

This compilation is dedicated to you and your dark.

Open the door, this entrance is for you.

Best enjoyed with a steaming beverage.

ACKNOWLEDGEMENT

Thank you to the repressed and creeping, you are finally free.

PREFACE

Because I must. And, with a must grows a dream. And dream morphs into an entity. And an entity sprouts horns. And horns pierce through the line we are trained to stay behind. Small steps, page by page – over the line.

ONE

ALONE I wait
In my cave of hate

Watching the swirl of stars
Hoping and dreaming of a falling Mars

Warring inside, splitting ends
But no one turns or bends

Alone I wait
How did I learn to hate

Wondering when the life will stop
No ladder to climb out the top

Well so deep
I cannot ground my sleep

Drowning in all this hate
Alone I wait

TWO

CLAWS of black, circles of hell
Bring them all to their cell

Sweet release and burning scent
Hallowed nothing, nothing meant

Dare of death, sweeping blow
Torture eminent, for the flow

Never more, even less
Crackle bone splattered mess

Lining up for their fate

  Peeling
  Decaying
  Dripping

Now become the bait
Consider the sin
But act too late

THREE

Sinister is …
the impreSsion
that somethIng EVIL
is happeNing
seeking to elIcit
your fearS
and That There is
SomEthing out there
That is HaRmful

FOUR

SENSATIONS high
Feelings plumet
Shut down
Shut down

Icy claws raking every thought
Riddled with masked intent
Paralyzed, choked out, suffocation
Fingers of knives closing in, regret

Open, blazing, frozen, death but alive
Inescapable, torture from within
Feed the demon, drown in agony together

Feed Feed feed

Ecstasy maximum, gliding and swirling, still
Knives slowly opening the grasp, air
Breathe easy, feelings glowing

Slowing slowing, slowing

Tightening, ending and landing the flight
Knives, Knives more jagged and tearing the
before

Use the Knives, slice the root, Feed with flood
Feed together, sweet release
Torture from within, grown by another
Gone and forgotten

FIVE

Remove the FLESH, see the bone
Thinner, thinner to make my own

Out out, measure the out
Complete the math, perfect the pout

Lonely lies, no matter the size
Slice and hack at my thighs

What do they think,
Make sure I, do not blink

See the bone fight this flesh
Only make it to their test

Free the bone
Trapped but not my own

SIX

SLEEPLESS sharp night-time

A golden, gapping rose weeps

Watching the thunder

SEVEN

Date
HATE
Mate
Donate
Create

No wait

Debate
Slate
Eliminate
Crate

No-weight

Backdate
Trait
Fixate

Checkmate

EIGHT

NEEDLE and thread
Needle and thread

Stitching the pieces back together with dread

Playing this game over and over
But never getting that clover

Playing this game of fear
Hoping to raise something different near

Catch the fever when all is done
Hoping to have more than just shun

Cradle of life, closed and withered
No entry, no admittance, no wizard

The pieces do not fit, stitch is closed
But we all play the game like we dozed

Wake up
Shake up
Plan for another break up

Stitching the pieces, never sound
Hope for another game, but never crowned

NINE

SLITHERING deep within the red
Eyes open and unblinking from under the bed

Hunger betrays and brings forth action
Facing down yet another faction

Screams ring out, but no one hears
Consuming hope, dreams and fears

Lay awake to stand the guard
Protect them, help them, share the shard

Stolen away and never returned
Broken, bloodied but none concerned

Another night, another feast
Am next or the least

TEN

Tear the flesh and REVEAL my truth
Peel the layers back and bare the bone
Twisting snaking becoming new

Bright and pale it brings my change
Prayer to the pale, prayer to the flesh
Gripping treading flight of feet

Hunt the hills dark and damp
Quench the thirst, snap and crunch
In the jaw on the mount

Freedom lies, chains of mind
Starving raging no control
Evidence left and hate grows

Wash away fear and tear again
Freedom of chains battle decides
Captured ended but sickness spreading

ELEVEN

The DARK
    Inky and black
    Heavy and not-slack
    Sneaking and lack
    Never coming back

The dim
    Grabbing and grim
    Bleak and trim
    Forever and skim
    Not on a whim

The dusk
    Charged and thick
    Dampened and slick
    Tumble and rick
    Shut down real quick

TWELVE

UNBENDING trusted

Surprisingly cold castle

Into the night flight

THIRTEEN

I SMILE down
Wearing my cloth crown

Friendly smile covers my lies
Bring them in, close their eyes

Build a net, feeling sound
Until I knock them off the mound

They do know the danger
Putting trust in this stranger

Friendly smile hides my jaw
Gnashing, biting, always gnaw

Tricking, trapping on my sly
Never caught, or I deny

I must feed
Must quench my need

Friendly smile
Its denial

FOURTEEN

Cruising through the FALSEHOOD
Making truths as you go
Punishing disobedience will an iron fist
Face value of health and guidance
Ulterior notions behind the fence

Clickity clack and swipe of the app
Control and divide
Practically a sacred outline
Place the thoughts and move the cash
Ownership to benefit the few

Freedom fabrications
Choice imitations

Charged to protect
Charged to grow

But only you will sow

FIFTEEN

What LURKED deep beneath the sparkle sheet

Large and looming, hungry, angry
Surfacing to the light

Dangling legs in the cool
Drawing nearer, searching more

The disturbance tracks even more
Nothing visible but you feel

Feel the change to the prey
Ignore the warning, stifle the panic

Look down deep at the mirror
One last breath, dragged to meet

Dangled legs gave a grip
Face to face with ancient instinct

Light fades, closing in
Terror warns, we should hear

What is beneath the sparkle sheet

SIXTEEN

Waiting, as I display the flesh
Holding tight covered by mesh

Wanting, the pleasure or the PAIN
Will they come and appease my gain

Pain of love, pleasure of grief

Need them both or have none
Without my demon I am done

Tear and torture the soft frame
Scars stay long but its my favourite game

Glutton more, bring your hate
It just develops it into great

Wish to trap you and give me emotion
I want to be your only devotion

Rip the heart, shred the soul
I will never be whole

Waiting, wanting
My favourite game

SEVENTEEN

Fear comes with a SPEAR
Its never cheer
And always near

Open hearts with a tear
        Could it become dear
        Passing from your peer

Maybe it can make it clear
        Helps you hear
        Helps you steer

Or its just simply with a sneer
        Surprise to appear
        Kicking into high gear

Savour or detest,
Fear will always come with a spear

EIGHTEEN

ARROWS, bows and sharpened knives
Zero all the lives

Hopeful voices plea in time
Praying they get to pay their dime

Scattered ashes, never found
Bring home the hidden and the bound

Crashing waves of hate inside
All because of the pride

Wasting, ripping taken every last
How can this be our past

Open festering rotten wounds
Carry forward to all the tunes

Forget and cover smokescreen lie
Drown the sorrow and help it die

Isolated and broken
Wounds that are never spoken

NINETEEN

COPE
  Nope

Hope
  Nope

Pope
  Nope

Down the slope
Try the rope

  Nope Nope Nope

I have lost my scope
And I can only mope

Can I try to cope

  Nope Nope Nope

TWENTY

Gliding SILENT through the night
Tracking lights for the flight

Found the small, blue sky rock
Long journey done, and we will not knock

Plans of wealth and fresh air signed
No dispute or chance for mankind

Cattle like and mindless drones
Won't be missed, tear down the stones

Primitive and hateful and for the better
Finally here now, follow the letter

Screams and pangs reach the skies
Calmness comes, no more cries

Cleanse complete, saved the day
Monsters are all put away

Notes to homes of our shear
All come now to the safe frontier

FINALE

Throughout THE pages, through the open door.
More thoughts hide on each shore:

ALONE the
CLAWS bring the
EVIL feeling new
SENSATIONS some of
FLESH some more bring
SLEEPLESS nights filled with
HATE need to use the
NEEDLE that stops the
SLITHERING only to
REVEAL what's in the
DARK you see an
UNBENDING glint a
SMILE covers the
FALSEHOOD hammered through has
LURKED and created so much
PAIN need to send
SPEARS and send
ARROWS into the heart but can never
COPE and never start
Silent waves in the night

Some may leave you without an oar.

www.ingramcontent.com/pod-product-compliance
Lightning Source LLC
Chambersburg PA
CBHW062206160726
48282CB00027B/1015
9789357617079